HEROES AND TRAITORS OF THE AMERICAN REVOLUTION

by Emma Carlson Berne

CAPSTONE PRESS
a capstone imprint

Published by Capstone Press, an imprint of Capstone
1710 Roe Crest Drive, North Mankato, Minnesota 56003
capstonepub.com

Library of Congress Cataloging-in-Publication Data is available on the Library of Congress website.
ISBN: 9798875254161 (hardcover)
ISBN: 9798875254116 (paperback)
ISBN: 9798875254123 (ebook PDF)

Summary: Narrative text looks at various people who influenced the American Revolution in order to understand multiple perspectives on history.

Editorial Credits: Editor: Mandy Robbins; Designer: Elijah Blue; Media Researcher: Rebekah Hubstenberger; Production Specialist: Tori Abraham

Image Credits
Associated Press: North Wind Picture Archives, 28; Bridgeman Images: 25, © North Wind Pictures, 5, Philadelphia History Museum at the Atwater Kent/Courtesy of Historical Society of Pennsylvania Collection, 7; Getty Images: Hulton Archive, 13, 16, Kean Collection, 21, MPI, 15, 17; Library of Congress: Prints & Photographs Division, cover, 12; National Archives and Records Administration: War Department. 1789-9/18/1947, 20; Newscom: Everett Collection, 23, Ken Welsh/ZUMA Press, 26; Shutterstock: kintore (globe icon), cover, 1, nik_nadal (search icon), cover, 1, Robert Plociennik (texture background), cover and throughout, Victorian Traditions, 18, Yuliia_Pizhivska (star border), cover and throughout; Smithsonian Institute: National Portrait Gallery; gift of the John Hay Whitney Collection, 11; The Metropolitan Museum of Art: Bequest of Adele S. Colgate, 1962, 9; The New York Public Library: Schomburg Center for Research in Black Culture, Manuscripts, Archives and Rare Books Division, 27

Printed and bound in China. 006459

TABLE OF CONTENTS

Words in **BOLD** are in the glossary.

Chapter 1

THE LEADERS

The 1760s and 1770s were a troubling time in the American colonies. From 1754 to 1763, Britain had fought the French and Indian War. They fought for more land in North America. Different groups of Native peoples fought on both sides too.

Britain won the war. But once it was over, the nation needed to pay for the costly war. The British government did this by placing taxes on the colonists. But the colonists had no representatives in the British government. They were angry at these increased taxes and their lack of control over them. By 1776, the Americans and the British were preparing to go to war.

King George

Both sides needed strong leaders. The British were ruled by both a king and Parliament. King George III had led Great Britain since 1760. He became king in the middle of the French and Indian War. After the war, King George supported the Native peoples in North America who had fought with the British. He set aside land for Native peoples. He ordered colonists not to settle there.

Angry colonists ripped down a statue of King George III.

King George believed that his government had the right to control the colonies. He ordered the British military to squash the rebellion. He did not want his leaders in North America to compromise with the rebels.

George Washington

George Washington was born in Virginia in 1732. He fought for the British in the French and Indian War. Washington was known for his bravery. During one battle, he had two horses shot out from under him, yet he continued to lead his men. He finished that battle with four bullet holes in his coat.

After the French and Indian War ended, Washington spoke out about the unfair treatment by the British. He represented Virginia at the First Continental Congress in 1774. This gathering of leaders met to debate whether the colonies should declare **independence** from Great Britain. Other leaders respected Washington's leadership. They admired his military knowledge too.

George Washington (in uniform) and two other representatives leave the First Continental Congress.

At the Second Continental Congress in 1775, colonial representatives chose Washington to lead the Continental Army. He did so for eight years. Washington took bold risks that eventually helped the United States win the war. He became a hero to the American people. Washington was the first person to sign the U.S. Constitution.

The American Revolution at a Glance

What?

The American Revolution (also called the Revolutionary War)

When?

1775–1783

Where?

New Hampshire, Massachusetts, Rhode Island, Connecticut, New York, New Jersey, Pennsylvania, Delaware, Maryland, Virginia, North Carolina, South Carolina, and Georgia.

Why?

- Discontent about taxes from the British government
- Lack of representation in Parliament
- Punishments the British placed on the colonists

After the Revolutionary War, the other leaders again asked Washington to step up. This time, they asked him to become the first president of the United States. He agreed. After eight years, George Washington said he was going to stop being president. This was unusual. Washington could have been president for the rest of his life. But he knew that the new United States needed to choose other leaders to help them grow as a country.

George Washington is sworn in as the first president of the United States.

Chapter 2

ON THE BATTLEFIELD

The battlefields of the American Revolution were bloody and chaotic. Leaders on both sides had to support their troops. At the same time, they had to make risky decisions. Courage, toughness, and smarts were required!

The Marquis de Lafayette

Gilbert du Motier, the Marquis de Lafayette, was from a rich, French noble family. He believed in the American cause and wanted to help them. Lafayette sailed to America and joined General Washington's forces. He fought in the Battle of Brandywine in Pennsylvania. He was shot in the leg. But he still led his soldiers as they retreated.

Because of the Marquis' bravery at Brandywine, George Washington made him a commander. Lafayette was dedicated to his soldiers. During the brutal winter of 1777 to 1778 at Valley Forge, he stayed with them in their huts. He spent his own money to buy them uniforms and weapons.

Lafayette returned to France in 1779. He arranged for 6,000 French troops to help the Americans. He commanded troops at the final battle of the war, the Battle of Yorktown. The French troops helped bring about the end of the war.

Marquis de Lafayette

FACT!

Continental commanders had slightly better living quarters at Valley Forge. They stayed in the houses of local farmers.

William Howe

General William Howe led the British forces. He often spoke out for fairer treatment of the American colonists. But his loyalty was with the Crown.

Howe had several victories during the war. His men defeated the patriots during the Battle of Bunker Hill in 1775. He led his troops to wins during the battles of Long Island, Brandywine, and Germantown. But Howe was blamed for the British losses at Valley Forge and Saratoga. Howe left his command in 1778.

General Howe

Charles Cornwallis

Before the war, General Charles Cornwallis was in British Parliament. He supported colonists during discussions in the British Parliament. He was one of only five members to vote against the Stamp Act, which taxed the colonists.

But when war broke out, Cornwallis commanded British troops. He led the capture of Fort Lee in November 1776. Cornwallis surrendered to American troops at the Battle of Yorktown. But he claimed to be sick during the surrender ceremony. He sent his second-in-command, Charles O'Hara, to sign the documents instead.

Cornplanter

The Seneca leader Cornplanter was born to a European father and a Seneca mother. He supported the British during the revolution. Cornplanter led his people in attacking settlements in New York and Pennsylvania.

After the revolution, Cornplanter switched sides and supported the Americans. He helped to **negotiate** three treaties with the new United States government. These treaties gave up large pieces of Native land. Cornplanter accepted a piece of land from the American government as payment for his help. He retired to his new land in Pennsylvania, where he lived the rest of his life.

FACT!

Cornplanter was also known as John O'Bail. His father had the same name. Cornplanter's two names reflect his two ancestries.

Cornplanter

Chapter 3

STATESMEN AND THINKERS

Some revolutionary leaders never came near a battlefield. Yet these diplomats and statesmen still influenced the outcome of the war. They helped create the path for the new United States.

Charles Townshend

British leader Charles Townshend created many of the taxes the colonists hated. He served in Parliament from 1747 to 1767. He was the author of the Townshend Acts. These laws demanded that Americans allow British officers into their homes. They also taxed items like lead, glass, and paper. Charles Townshend died in 1767. He didn't live to see the American Revolution. But he helped to cause it.

Charles Townshend

Thayendanegea (Joseph Brant)

Thayendanegea was a Mohawk chief who supported the British. He led discussions among the **Iroquois Confederacy**. They talked about the Native people's role in the revolution. He declared that the Mohawks would support the British. This idea split the nations of the Confederacy. Thayendanegea led Native fighters throughout the war. Afterward, the British gave him and his people land in Canada. Today this area is known as Brantford.

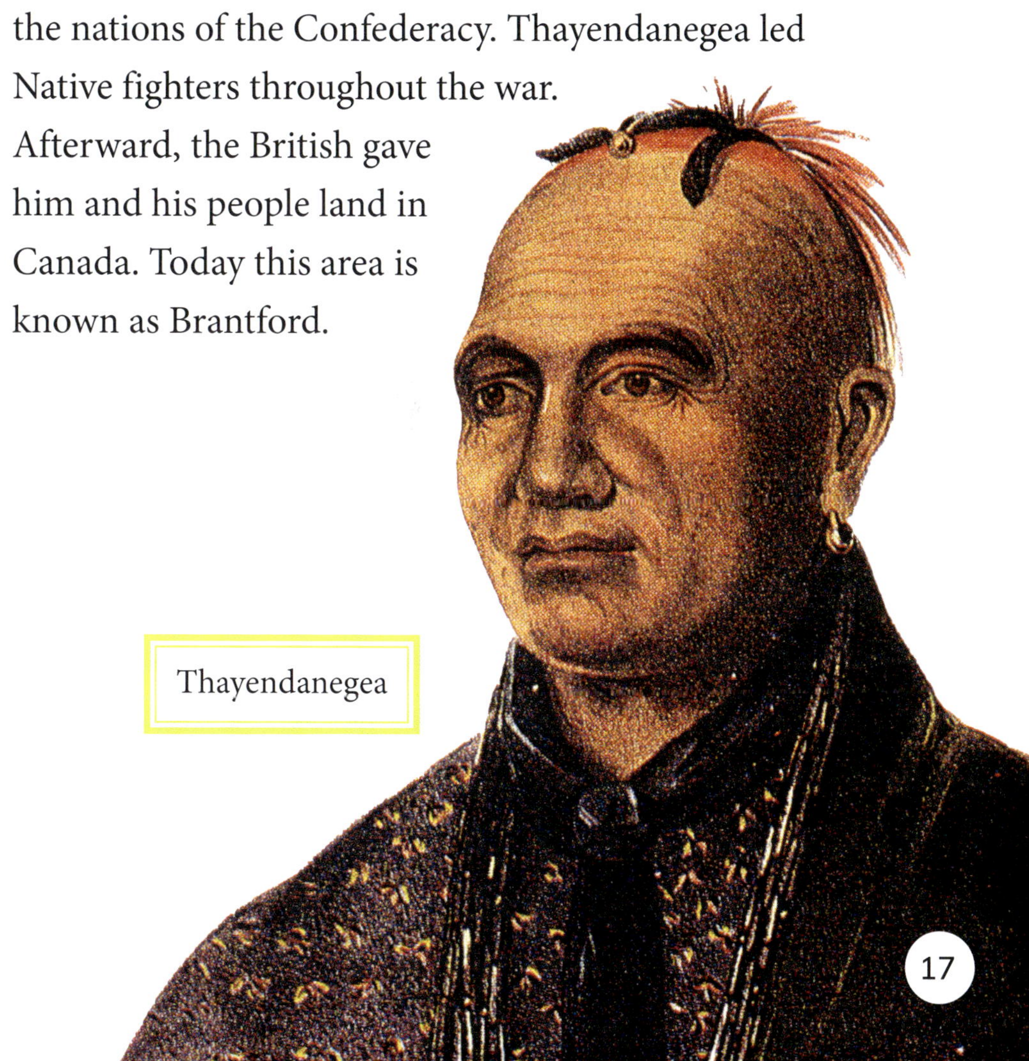

Thayendanegea

Benjamin Franklin

Benjamin Franklin was a printer, a scientist, and an inventor. He represented Pennsylvania at the Second Continental Congress. During that important meeting, Franklin helped develop the plan for the revolution. He and the other leaders decided where troops would be and when. They picked commanders. Later, Franklin helped write and signed the Declaration of Independence.

Franklin spent 1776 to 1778 in France. There, he convinced the French to support American independence. With French money and military support, the Americans defeated the British. After the British surrendered, Franklin helped to negotiate the peace treaty for the new American government.

Franklin (left), John Adams (center), and Thomas Jefferson (right) working on the Declaration of Independence

Revolutionary War Timeline

April 1775	The first battles at Lexington and Concord occur.
May 1775	The Continental Congress votes to form the Continental Army with Washington as its leader.
June 1775	The Battle of Bunker Hill is won by the British, who suffer heavy casualties.
March 1776	The Continental Army pushes the British out of Boston.
July 1776	The Continental Congress votes to adopt the Declaration of Independence.
Sept. 1776	New York falls under British control.
Dec. 1776	The Continental Army captures Trenton after crossing the Delaware River.
Sept.-Oct. 1777	The Americans win the Battle of Saratoga.
Dec. 1777	The Continental Army begins a long, cold encampment at Valley Forge in Pennsylvania.
Feb. 1778	France enters the war as an American ally against the British.
Oct. 1781	The British army loses the Battle of Yorktown and surrenders to the Continental Army. The United States wins the war.
Sept. 3, 1783	The Revolutionary War is officially over with the signing of the Treaty of Paris.

Alexander Hamilton

Alexander Hamilton was George Washington's secretary during the war. He also led troops at the Battle of Yorktown. He was born on a tiny Caribbean island. After a hurricane destroyed most of his community, Hamilton wrote an impressive letter about it that was published in a newspaper. People thought he was a great writer. They collected money to send him to school in the United States.

Once in America, Hamilton became a lawyer. During the war, he begged George Washington to let him command troops. Washington finally did. Hamilton led his men to a victory at Yorktown. After the war, Hamilton helped write the Constitution. He was one of the founders of the American financial system and the first Secretary of the Treasury.

Alexander Hamilton

Thomas Jefferson

Thomas Jefferson was a writer, a founding father, and the third president of the United States. At the Second Continental Congress, Jefferson was chosen to be the main writer of the Declaration of Independence. He combined ideas from literature and philosophy in the document. Jefferson gave the other leaders a draft of the Declaration of Independence on June 28, 1776. The leaders edited and debated it. Then they voted to adopt it on July 4, 1776.

Chapter 4

TRAITORS AND SPIES

Neither side could get by without spies. These men and women risked their lives to gather information and pass messages. **Traitors** who switched sides often brought valuable knowledge too. Loved or hated, traitors and spies were an important part of the revolution.

Benedict Arnold

General Benedict Arnold started his military career as a patriot. He was a member of the Sons of Liberty. This group organized the Boston Tea Party. When the revolution began, Arnold joined the Connecticut **militia**. He fought in the Siege of Boston and the Battle of Saratoga. Arnold helped to capture Fort Ticonderoga and was promoted to general. George Washington thought of him as one of his strongest leaders.

But Arnold was angry when he was not promoted to major general as soon as he had wanted. He argued with other high-ranking officers. Eventually, Arnold began telling American war secrets to the British. In 1780, his spying was discovered. He was accused of being a traitor. He switched sides and began leading British troops. Benedict Arnold died in England in 1801.

Benedict Arnold

Benjamin Church

Benjamin Church was a member of the Sons of Liberty. But in 1775, a letter between Church and General Thomas Gage, leader of the British forces, was found. The letter was written in code. Once it was decoded, the patriots realized Church had been a spy since 1772.

Ann Bates

Ann Bates was a schoolteacher who also worked as a loyalist spy. Her husband was a British soldier. Bates would disguise herself as a **peddler** and enter American army camps. There, Bates noted how many men, cannons, and other weapons the Americans had. She would report back to the British about what she'd seen. Ann Bates was arrested for spying around 1778. When she was released from jail, Bates continued spying. Eventually, the information she gathered caused the British to send more troops to Newport, Rhode Island. American troops retreated.

Robert Townsend

Tavern owner Robert Townsend presented himself as a loyalist. He even wrote for a loyalist newspaper. But Townsend was a patriot spy. British officers spoke freely to him in his tavern. He noted the information and passed it along to the Americans.

Continental soldiers in camp before the Battle of Yorktown

FACT!

Washington and his spies often passed messages using invisible ink.

Benjamin Tallmadge

Benjamin Tallmadge was George Washington's master spy. In 1778, he created the Culper Spy Ring in New York City. Tallmadge **recruited** his friends to find useful information and pass it along.

Tallmadge created a special number code that spies used throughout the war. He also passed information to Washington that helped American forces capture the city of Newport, Rhode Island.

Benjamin Tallmadge

James Fayette

James Fayette was an enslaved man who volunteered for the Continental Army. As a spy, Fayette worked as a double agent. He told the British he would spy on the patriots for them. But in fact, Fayette was spying on the British. He was collecting useful information. He reported that information back to the patriots. Information that Fayette gathered helped Washington win at the Battle of Yorktown. This battle ended the war.

James Fayette

FACT!

American spy Nathan Hale was caught and hanged by the British. According to legend, his last words were, "I only regret that I have but one life to give for my country."

Hercules Mulligan and Cato

Hercules Mulligan was a **tailor** and patriot soldier and spy. He and Cato, a man enslaved by Mulligan, gathered information from British officers who came to the tailor shop. As the soldiers had their uniforms sewn, Mulligan would chat with them. He would ask them when they needed their uniforms back. This way, he could figure out when the British troops were going to be moving.

Cato would ride out to George Washington's headquarters with the news. At one point, a British officer had demanded his coat back in a rush. He let it slip that he was going to capture George Washington the next day. Cato immediately set out with the information. It saved Washington's life. It might have saved the American cause altogether.

Overlapping Roles

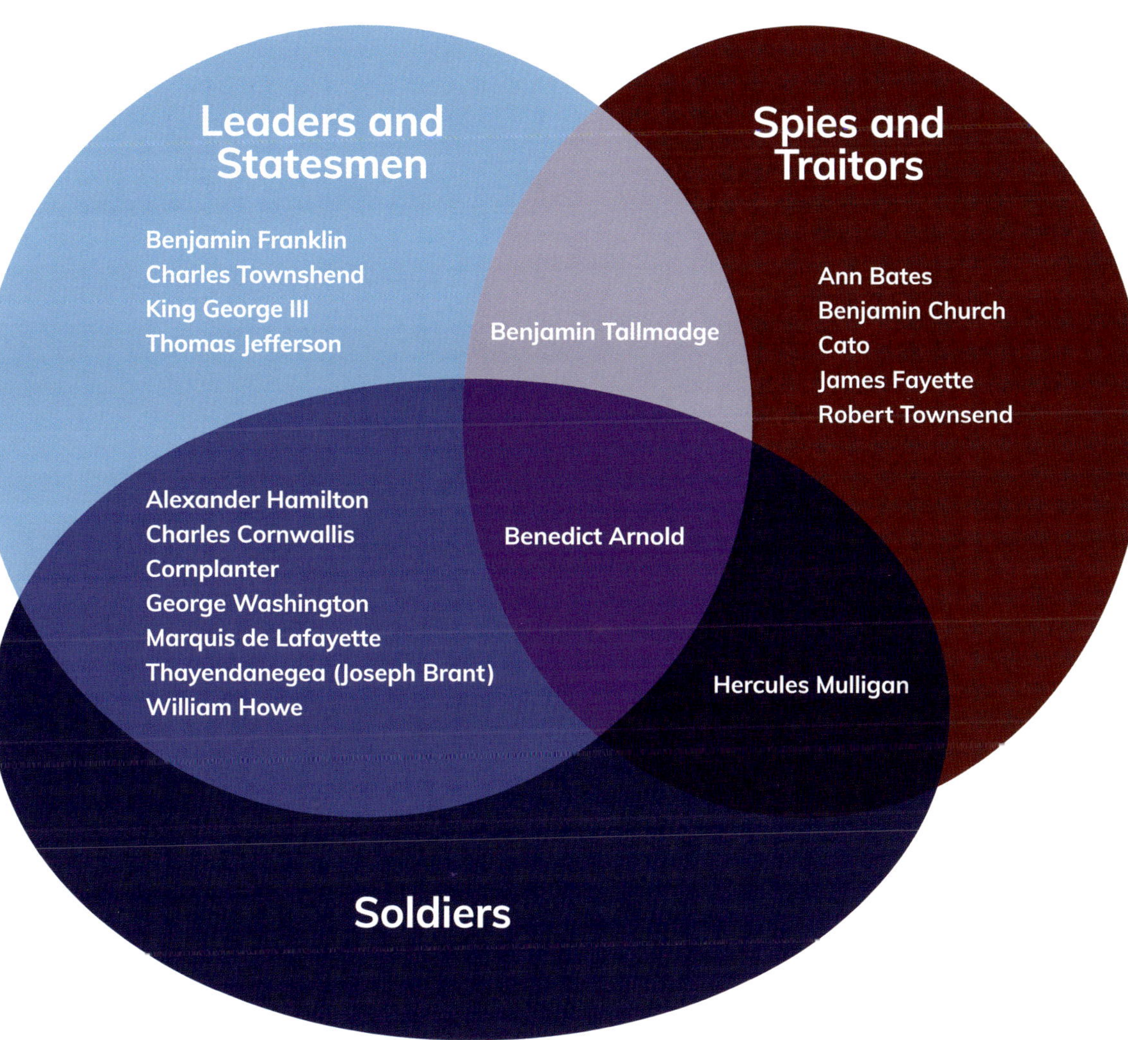

Glossary

independence (in-di-PEN-duhnss)—freedom from the control of other people or things

Iroquois Confederacy (IHR-uh-koy kuhn-FE-druh-see)—a political alliance and cultural community of several Native American tribes in what is now upper New York state and southeastern Canada

militia (muh-LISH-uh)—a group of volunteer citizens organized to fight, but who are not professional soldiers

negotiate (ni-GOH-shee-ate)—to bargain or discuss something to come to an agreement

peddler (PED-luhr)—a person who travels around selling things

recruit (ri-KROOT)—to seek out someone for a job

tailor (TAY-luhr)—a person whose job it is to make or alter clothing

traitor (TRAY-tur)—someone who aids the enemy of their country

Read More

DK Eyewitness: American Revolution. New York: DK, 2022.

Kawa, Katie. *George Washington and Alexander Hamilton*. New York: Gareth Stevens, 2022.

London, Martha. *Revolutionary War Spy Stories*. North Mankato, MN: Child's World, 2021.

Internet Sites

The Founding Fathers
kids.britannica.com/kids/article/Founding-Fathers/627390

Hands-on-History: Spies in the American Revolution
edit.mountvernon.org/plan-your-visit/calendar/events/hands-on-history-spies-in-the-american-revolution

History for Kids: The American Revolution
historyforkids.org/american-revolution-facts-information-for-kids/

Index

About the Author

Emma Carlson Berne has written many books for young readers. She lives in Cincinnati, Ohio, with her husband, three boys, one grumpy cat, and one friendly cat.